Drunk in Sunlight

For Mark,

With gratitude and,
as always, great affection.
Looking forward to seeing
you more frequently on
either end of the
interstate. (I-65)

Danny
July, 2007

Daniel Anderson

JOHNS HOPKINS:
POETRY AND FICTION
John T. Irwin
General Editor

Drunk in Sunlight

Daniel Anderson (signature)

THE JOHNS HOPKINS
UNIVERSITY PRESS
Baltimore

This book has been brought to publication with the
generous assistance of the Albert Dowling Trust.

The Johns Hopkins University Press
2715 North Charles Street
Baltimore, Maryland 21218-4363

www.press.jhu.edu

Library of Congress Cataloging-in-Publication Data

Anderson, Daniel, 1964–
    Drunk in sunlight / Daniel Anderson.
        p. cm. — (Johns Hopkins, poetry and fiction)
    ISBN 0-8018-8520-5 (acid-free paper) — ISBN 0-8018-8521-3
(pbk. : acid-free paper)
    I. Title. II. Series.
    PS3551.N3584D78 2007
    811'.54—DC22   2006010574

A catalog record for this book is available from the British Library.

for Hilary,
her laughter
and her love

Contents

Acknowledgments

I would like to thank the editors of the following magazines, in which some of these poems first appeared: *Alabama Literary Review*: "On Having Said Something Cruel" and "Reading History"; *The Carolina Quarterly*: "Aubade," "First Frost," and "High School Reunion, 1998"; *The Cincinnati Review*: "Bill Fowler's Pointer Hears a Voice," "Probability and Statistics," "Question," and "Cycling"; *Crab Orchard Review*: "In Here. Out There." (originally printed as "At Three A.M."); *The Formalist*: "Rising Tide at Schoodic Point"; *The Hudson Review*: "In Minnesota Once," "Sea Glass"; *The Kenyon Review*: "The Wasp That's Lately Died"; *New England Review*: "Early Autumn in Tennessee," "Elegy for the Dying Dog," and "We've Gathered in a Formal Garden"; *Poetry*: "À la Belle Étoile"; *River Styx*: "America the Beautiful" and "Burning the House"; *Southern Cultures*: "The Pond in Summertime"; *Southwest Review*: "O, Florida"; *The Southern Review*: "Sunflowers in a Field"; *The Yale Review*: "Returning Home Late Sunday Night." "Thorns.Thistles." was first published in *The Kenyon Review* and reprinted in *Pushcart Prize XXX: Best of the Small Presses*.

I also wish to express my gratitude to the Bogliasco Foundation and the National Endowment for the Arts for fellowships I received while writing these poems. For the Kenan Visiting Writer position and the Nancy and Rayburn Watkins Endowed Professorship in Creative Writing, I would like to thank the University of North Carolina at Chapel Hill and Murray State University, respectively, whose generous appointments allowed me the time and peace of mind to work. Thanks as well to John Irwin for his interest in this book and his editorial insights. "Question" is for John Hollander who once remarked, "poetry notices." Finally, I owe a great debt to the benevolent spirit of Tennessee Williams, whose bequest to the University of the South has led to many opportunities for me; among these I would include a number of summers spent in Sewanee as well as four very happy years of teaching there.

I

Returning Home Late Sunday Night

Pale bulb. High sun. At Friday noon
The porch lamp seemed a minor waste,
But in the intervening days
A darkness has replaced
My bright backyard. The weed-cracked drive
Advances into nothingness.
It's queer, perhaps too simple, how,
Returning home late Sunday night,
That light burns like a stroke of genius now,
Elucidating moths, a rusted chair,
The gate that bears a jaw of shadowed fangs,
And a spider's needlework in which
The small, shriveled skeletons of flies
Decay. Like props abandoned from a play,
Two unread papers languish in the grass.

Gravel. Latch. Hinge and lock. Each noise
Grows amplified. Then suddenly it seems
Not just a weekend but a decade lost.
There is a flavor of frost, the cloud-scrubbed moon,
The rush of something dreadful yet to come,
Not sleet nor snowflake on the mounting wind,
But soon.

Sunflowers in a Field

Sunflowers in a field.
Goldfinches everywhere.
They gorge on seed. They rise
To rest along the power line, then fall
Like drizzled lemon drops, like lozenges
Of candied yellow light.
Two weeks a year, goldfinches
Gather on sunflowers here.
These evenings after supper,
You see them in the honey-soft glow
As if they'd trapped and somehow stored
The rapture of September's sun.
You see goldfinches flicker
Among sunflower lanes,
Through mortal tides of light,
Through streams of apricot and chardonnay,
And you resolve to live
Your life with greater sympathy.
Sunflowers bowing their char-black dials,
Their petals twist and writhe
Like fires, like silk coronas blazing west.
How inconceivable then,
The pewter-making cold-front clouds,
The shabby settlement of crow and wren.
Though no one hears the oath,
You shall, you tell yourself,
Forego deceit, increase the tithe.
Atone. Forgive. Embrace. You watch
Goldfinches and sunflowers both
Begin to fade. By subtle green degrees

They shed that bullion luster of the sun
Until the finches ricochet
Like flints among the drowsing flower heads.
Perhaps, as I have done,
You'll pace the darkening half mile home,
Intent on picking up the telephone
To reconcile with long-lost friends.
You will apologize, concede.
You'll vow to never, ever, ever let
Such distance grow again.
But then you reach your door and find
The day diminished to a thin blue rind
Of light above the township silhouette.
How nice a hot bath sounds.
Dessert. An herbal tea.
Perhaps you'll read the Arts
And Leisure pages of the daily news.
With every stair you climb
Sleep settles just a little more behind
The knees, beneath the shoulder blades.
The calls, you tell yourself,
Perhaps some other time.

Elegy for the Dying Dog

Tomorrow he will die.
For now, though, see him drowsing in the shade.
A cardinal cracks the red whip of its flight.
Frail butterflies—the metalmark,
the spicebush swallowtail—are lobbed
like painted tissue on the air.
The wind, as it might carve on fields of wheat,
Combs over his black coat. I've set him there
As water irises prepare
Their gold unfolding in the rain-fresh pond.
Last meal: Steamed rice. Grilled strips of steak.
Last lazy afternoon. Last hour
To watch the clouds drift like meringues,
To watch them blended into tones of peach
Then deepen to the dusky tints of plums.
One last command to heed or disobey,
But it's not me who's calling Virgil now,
It's Death who's calling, calling, calling,
And he comes.

Thorns. Thistles.

Three starlings jig and sprint,
Teasing the sprinkler's oscillating spray
That pulses like a sterling macramé
Of water on the lawn.
If actuaries are to be believed,
Barring unforeseen circumstances,
I have, roundly, two thousand Saturdays
To live. Four hundred waning crescent moons,
Some thirty-seven more Thanksgiving meals,
And nine elections for the President.
In the rich, blue, waxing alp of shade
The gabled roof has laid,
The lilies cool. The lilies bruise.
Now, by my own accounts, I'd guess
Almost twelve thousand shaves,
Six thousand hours, more or less,
Of watching televised athletics,
And five hundred ventures—give or take—
To haul the empty bottles to the dump.
In five o'clock's thin light,
All multiples of green begin to blur.
Mulberry bush. The buckeye. The ivy vines.
A nearby power mower whines
In Doppler modulation, like locust-song.
It floats this precinct of the middle class
With the sweet, cut scent of grass,
And nothing, nothing now, seems wrong.
Three hundred thirty books of stamps,
Two hundred airline flights,
Ninety dental appointments,

Seven timing belts, and three more dogs.
Two times a year, or so,
(Which roughly comes to seventy in all)
I'll cry myself to sleep.
My, how our silver willows weep.
The tulips lift their chalice heads
As in a crimson toast.
L'chaim! they seem to say, or *Skoal!*
I have, I'd speculate,
One hundred sixty-five of these
Late-day harmonic moments left—
Of iced tea and the Adirondack chair,
Of pure and undistracted ease,
Until a car horn's blare,
Or the gun-crack slamming of a back porch door,
The day's commotion coming home at last.
One hundred sixty-four.

Burning the House

All afternoon and into Tuesday night
We watched them burn the skeletal remains
Of Webster's place. The whole house growled with heat.
The windows seethed. And when the winds reversed
Bright bursts of sparks were peppered high above
The corner of Magnolia Street and First,
Where we stray neighbors gathered on our way
From work, from school, and play. Two months ago
They found the Websters' bodies side by side,
Almost untouched by fire. They died, we said,
As emblems—figures of eternal love
Who perished in each other's arms. Since then,
Some vandals busted out their glass and sprayed
A fresh vocabulary on their walls.
Homecoming week, someone strung an effigy
Of Lincoln from their ancient apple tree.
Our sixteenth president in pads and cleats.
So council took a vote, condemned the lot,
And set the razing date for Tuesday last.

We stopped, turned up our collars on the chill,
Not thinking of the family but the fire,
That radiating heat and smell of char,
The cozy snap-snap-snapping of the flames.
Then most of us continued on for home.
We left each beam and joist, each plank and sash,
The sundry small possessions of a life,
Disintegrating piecemeal into ash.
Things seemed a little different for a day,

The cold commuters shuffling off to work,
The primal cry of each departing train,
And where the Websters lived for forty years,
Two chimneys rising in the Wednesday rain.

The Wasp That's Lately Died

She came late yesterday to find
This window latched against the April air,
And soon forgetting how she'd pinched between

The battered screen and warped wood of the sash,
Began to thrash against the glass until,
All venom of her hot temper spent,

She lay exasperated on the sill.
So there! We sometimes like to say,
Another quarrel with the world gone cold.

Her velvet abdomen become a scab.
The crisp wind whittles her. She's now no more
Alarming than some scraps of marigold,

So lately dried and fallen from their flower.
But this means little to the gypsy moth
That beats his single-minded self against

The kitchen pane, explodes in flight,
Relaxes then explodes again.
It will go on like this all night.

Early Autumn in Tennessee

Before October's gold veneer
Of leaf has covered the chilled creek,
And all the trees have grown antique
With change, before the wind unveils
Each rickety and grim physique
Of maple, poplar, oak, and elm,
The cotton downs the drying field
Like strange, anachronistic snow.
The monarchs come. The monarchs go.
But still there are late swallowtails,
The cloudless sulfurs, too, that glow
Like incandescent lemon skins.
Just yesterday the evening sky
Grew gas blue like a pilot light.
The meadow purpled into night.
And as a flock of grackles came
The black confetti of their flight
Seemed suddenly to shape a slurred,
Profoundly large and fleeting word
Against the cool and fragile dusk.
At the meadow's far end I heard
The downward spiraling of song.
It was a screech owl's shrill reply
To what was written on the clear sky,
Though, really, who could comprehend
The meaning of that mournful cry?
The air was sweet with soil and hay.
Two jet trails hooked a loose crochet
Across the writhing apple green
And phlox blue of the dying day.

It was a feeling more than a thought
That those cold colors smoldering there
Seemed like the colors of despair
Or some unnamable regret.
While such forebodings, it is true,
Will seldom sway the courts of law
Or topple legislative chambers,
They may give prophets pause, or make
The broken-hearted exiles weep,
And this, for many, is enough.

II

Reading History

When the president is overthrown and parliament dissolved,
When cabinet ministers are jailed, it will occur to them,
Though briefly so, to gather their assets in haste
And flee. When fool and laureate are hanged, the daughters raped,
When all that was forbidden once—the carnage and the lust—
Becomes the order of the day, they will adjust.
How strangely, then, their happiness will seem remote.
They will relinquish livestock, the lands, and the good view,
Those mild pastures, the forests, and the clear trout streams.
They will no longer calculate the rate of their returns,
Summer by the lake, or stroke the dog's soft jaw at dusk.
Nor will they take their drinks at six—the cool tonics with lime.
They will remember how one sunny day in June
The constable addressed a crowded briefing room
To reassure the press the bloody crackdown would resume.
That all belongs to a different time, a different dream,
For the royalist supporters of the previous regime.

Dimensions, Senses, Affections

*And I will give unto thee, and to thy
seed after thee, the land wherein
thou art a stranger.*

Genesis 17:8

I

Behold the carrot cake, the coffee cake,
The onion, and translucent strips of lox.
Scent the aromatic and greasy steam
Of kugel, quiche, and potato knish.
See how the salmon trains his eye
On the buttermints and stacks of marbled rye.
Your loud-mouthed cousin cracking jokes
Will be here on the holidays.
Just listen to his rowdy voice
Above the mild clatter of the crowd.
Get used to him. The confidence
In his aggressive laugh insists
That sometimes love is not a choice.
But even he can't shake you from your sleep.
The mohel rubs your lips with wine.
He tells us you will feel a sudden smart,
And though it may be difficult to bear
We must remember that your cries will pass.
All pains, he tells us, are deciduous.

II

On Moriah, Isaac watched his father shape
An altar, he saw him rack the wood
And fan the blue smoke into flame.

And Isaac asked his father then
Why they should build that consecrated fire
When they had nothing for their burnt offering.
"My son, God will provide himself a lamb."
These were the words of ancient Abraham
Who had no other choice. Who knew
But could not say to Isaac, "It is you,
My true begotten child, our sacrifice."

III
Almighty, watchful Adonai.
Great author of the arbitrary laws.
Indifferent architect of grief,
Of exponential joy. The mastermind.
All-potent pedagogue behind
An Ivy League curriculum in loss,
In anger, ecstasy, regret, and love,
Who teaches us to feel, at times, alone,
At times, unbearably misunderstood,
To feel the unrelenting knucklebone
Of what it means to be a Jew,
Not orthodox, exultant, or devout,
But what I really mean to say is this:
Who hasn't thought himself to be, at times,
One of a chosen, isolated few?
So utterly contested in his faith,
Dispersed at random, driven out?
Witness, God, the covenant,
And if, above the earthly din,
If over every solitary cry,
You hear this prayer, take notice of the day.
Protect the child from fang and claw,

The madness of his time, the fatal flaw.
Be ever-gentle with his résumé.

IV

Sawyer Caleb Freeman, hear the laugh
Of someone joking in the other room.
Inhale the complicated blend
Of French perfume and aftershave,
Of coffee brewing in a polished urn.
The brave parade before your eyes,
Of florid blouses, scarves, and silken ties,
Meanders like a psychedelic stream
That shimmers, billows, ebbs, and blurs.
The mohel rubs your lips with wine.
It may be difficult to bear at first.
It will not last. But wawl and shriek.
Remind us how the empty air
Is crammed with promise, platitude, and truth.
And teach us once again, the worldly wise,
Who hear but cannot ease your cries, that love,
Dear Sawyer, always (always) breaks the heart.

Cycling

for Michael Rosenhaus

Today, on Sugar Dairy Road,
I pumped. I cranked and pedaled past
The old tobacco barn, the bleached white church
And all its lurching, weather-beaten graves.
I slugged it up the stubborn hill,
And swept the hairpin corner falcon-fast.
But what I'd have you understand
Is not the labor or the sweat
Of someone courting early middle age
Who, in the glory of his mind,
Pretends he's racing through the alps,
Or that he's left the peloton behind.
I'd have you take your rest instead,
Inhale that sharp wild onion air,
And let the bloodbeat thunder in your chest.
Behold the pure high-voltage flight
Of Eastern bluebirds where they pass
Above the cattle grazing in the grass,
Then spend themselves across the meadow's rise
Beyond dual silver silos. Champagne dry
Light breezes stir the drifts and squalls
Of cherry blossom snow. Do I
Believe in something like the soul
Or the sublime? On most days I'd say no.
But then the look of certain art—
Lithe, waving grains. A sourceless glow—
Might settle on a pasture side,
Or late at night with friends I'll feel

The sudden whipcrack clarity of love,
And then I'm almost sure. Today,
The nectar-yellow light, that shade
Mulberrying the roadside where I stood,
The meadow's green, like billiard-table felt,
These swayed me once again. Although my faiths,
By standards of the faithful, may be brief,
I stopped a while, grown absolutely drunk
On something. Something like belief.

Question

The Genius of Poetry must work out its own salvation in man:
It cannot be matured by law and precept, but by sensation and
watchfulness—

Keats

You've seen this all somewhere before,
An ancient Mycenaean stamp
Of sunlight that shellacks the lake.

The reeds. The coupling dragonflies,
Unbearably breakable and blue.
Is this a ghost of summer camp?

Some gilded August day in Maine
Come once again to stir an ache?
The poem comprehends. It tries

To name this mild, nostalgic view,
And, if you let it, will express
A vagrant everlastingness.

The poem sees two dragonflies.
They scrawl their brutal script against
The breeze. Steel cursives. Neon scrolls.

Their evanescent sentence wisps
Away. The poem hears a splash.
It scans the insect-stippled air.

It glances down to see a chilled
And silver chaos published there.
In those glints of the shattered sky,

Those ribs of water shuttling out,
The poem, having missed the trout
Exploding for the circling fly,

Sees not the lake's embossed veneer
But rather other things grown clear.
A childhood bliss. A puzzling dream.

A lately recollected lie.
These glimmer in the poem's ken
As dandled, sunstruck prisms might.

Poem, what will you make of them?
What of the lily pads and trees
That ride the water's wine-dark mirror?

The dragonflies, they come again
Like blue allusions, silks of thought.
They jostle, tease, and occupy

The strangest quarters of your mind,
Enchanting, sometimes troubling, too,
The restless province of your eye.

À la Belle Étoile

It's late. Even our flight attendants drowse,
And twenty thousand feet below
Vermont is pillowed safely in snow.

Across that dove-gray nether world
A nightshift worker navigates her car,
Her headlights veering like a ruined star

Toward several cottages that house
Mysterious and forbidden lives.
What is it that we see out there,

We sleepless passengers who stare
Where the moon and pewter clouds carouse?
Or on the starboard aisle, who eye

Those shifting galaxies and nebulae—
Star-dusted, far-off Syracuse,
Rochester glittering, and Buffalo?

Some read detective novels, some
The lacquered glamour ads in magazines,
While others study lace and fern

Of frost feathering the Plexiglas.
Cleveland, Mansfield, then Columbus pass
Like cities winter-deep in fireflies.

"O my good gosh! Millinocket Lake?"
A woman's gingham voice behind us cries.
"*We* used to spend *our* summers there!"

"I hate to say this but the world *is* small,"
The liver-spotted man beside her sighs.
And maybe you can nearly start to see

Old Millinocket Lake, the family camp
Where it is always 1963,
July and smoky and a little damp.

The cabin is tobacco-dark inside,
Fishing tackle tangled at its door,
Sand sprinkled on its thinly varnished floor.

All day the oscillating fan's blade
Nick-nick-nicking at its metal cage,
Grandfather on the dock at his easel,

Painting the children in their birch canoe.
Snapdragon-yellow sun. Trees, beetle green.
Such north Atlantic rarities in blue.

Our destination smolders into view,
A phosphorescent cluster on the south,
And Millinocket goes the way

Of each refinery and farm,
Each tinseled hamlet over which we've flown.
Our Boeing dips its wing. We hear the high

Accelerating whine, the chuck
And grumble of the landing gear.
Then suddenly the cosmic and the vast

Sharpen to particulars at last.
Those candelabra, that bright chandelier,
The distant cigarette and awl

Enlarge as through a looking glass
To vacant lot and spot-lit salvage yard,
Smokestack and the Methodist spire.

Warehouses ribbed with razor wire
Are haloed in a carbide glow.
Yet even from here, this simple height,

This jurisdiction of the common crow,
The inexplicable, unjust, and sad
Seem comfortably nestled among

The paisley, checkerboard, and plaid
Façade of Nashville, Tennessee,
Where just a little while from now

The clenched young woman sitting next to me
Will walk the beige and hollow length
Of her apartment building hall,

Jangle her copper keys, and formulate
The very last thing she should have said—
Exact and ruthless—to her new

Ex-lover sleeping soundly in his bed
This time of night in ice-bound Montreal
Where she would rather be instead.

The Pond in Summertime

Thin drifts of pollen floated on the air,
And through a galaxy of flies
I watched small fish, like silver muscles, rise,
Convulse, then wriggle quickly down.
The burgundy complexion of the pond
Had mostly blistered up in green.
I wouldn't swim because I was afraid
Of the snapping turtle and the sly snake.
No matter if they were not there,
The mind would always see them there.
My cousin Mary peeled her sandals off,
Stripped down to her blue bathing suit,
And dove into the amniotic deep.
When she came slogging out, her legs
And arms were crazed with muddy rivulets.
Her suit was bruised with dabs of olive foam.
I was eleven, maybe twelve.

Today a key-lime lather spreads across
The pond. A different pond. And I think *yes,*
The cattails look like riding crops.
And I think *yes,* the lush lily pads.
The armored stalks of thistle. Breaching bass.
And I think *Mary Satterfield.*
Fleet swallows skim the pond. They prick
The marbled water with their beaks.
They flitter off. They prick again.
That's right, I think, *her daughter Katy, too.*
Both dead some twenty years by Mary's hand.
And if, today, I cannot quite

Remember her, she's all these things at once:
The cobalt blue of dragonflies.
Mail Pouch barns. Southeast Ohio Summer.
The hot blacktop outside the Dairy Freeze.
She is a fraying white electric thread
Of lightning on a coming cloud,
The nearby thunderclap and sudden storm.
First crush. First funeral. The undiscussed.
A whispered family name. Just one
Of several hundred Adams County graves.
She is the lexicon of August trees,
The hi-watt surge on an AM radio,
A car that smelled of cigarettes and rain.

Old Stone Houses

What leavens them? Whatever makes
This commonwealth of grackles rise and scroll
Across the pasture's February blond?
They bank and roll

And in their frenzy fan themselves
Into a smokeless, towering black flame,
Or something like a Pentecostal tongue
Whose cryptic name

For rapture will evaporate
The bright, split-second after it is said.
How ruthlessly they shape the billowed sail
And arrowhead,

Or the stippled image of a fish
Leaping into a pool of nothingness.
They flurry there awhile and come about
To sway and bless

The blanched white of the winter air,
Then sweep the stranded tractor and its plough,
The horseless, parched corral and battered trough.
Cascading now

Over a phantom ledge of shale,
They ride the windward pleasure of their will
Until they spill like far-flung apple seed
On Washburn's hill,

Though they are not at rest for long
Before they startle, nervously combust,
And pepper lower heaven once again.
Each crumpling gust

Urging them further out of view,
Blunt beads at first, then finer points compressed
Against the cumbersome and deepening
Jam-colored west

Where old stone houses have begun
To stamp their brooding silhouettes. Light blooms,
However apprehensively, in side
And upper rooms

In which I should suppose there are
Unanswered letters, diaries, bouquets
Of dried wildflowers on the bureau tops,
The prim displays

Of crystal knickknacks on the shelves,
And now and then some man or woman who,
At having felt a draft, decides to pull
The curtains to,

But not before the long last gaze
Into a brief bewilderment of snow
Where coal-black grackles mapped the eggshell sky
Moments ago.

This is the way it ends sometimes,
The day grown flat and lusterless as tin.
And this is true both looking out, I think,
And looking in.

III

Rising Tide at Schoodic Point

Before the fabulous display,
As when a Roman candle thuds,
The wave will rush the black basalt,
Draw back, unleash a *boom!* then vault
Its sunstruck rhapsody of suds,
A violent billowing of spray

That for a moment climbs the air
And hurls its protozoic mass,
Refuses gravity until,
However quickly, it seems to still
A frozen showering of glass,
And then begins a debonair

Collapse. Its baubles, polished stones,
Fistfuls of agates spryly tossed,
All vanish into soapy blinks.
One thinks of Tiffany or Brinks
To see this wealth of foam and frost
Crash down like crystal sparrows' bones.

The whole thing shatters on the rocks.
And what is left? A creamy lake.
A loose, unraveling bolt of lace
That wavers on the ocean's face.
Then in the carbonated wake,
Which saturates those amber locks

Of ocean weed, a misty squall
Evaporates above the sea.
The waters warp, retreat, and then
Those emerald currents surge again
In a diamond-studded filigree.
See how these fortunes rise and fall.

What holds us here more than the float
Of jade and water-gust? One might
Conclude both terror and a bliss,
Much like a first uncertain kiss
That fills the sternum with delight
And clutches—slightly—at the throat.

In Minnesota Once

Consider how the light rain falls,
How imperceptibly the water beads
A row of gems along the gutter's lip.
Fat diamonds dollop down then bloom
Again. For days late spring's relentless mist
Has turned the underbark of birches black,
And everywhere the spastic code of Morse
Is tapped on shingles, leaves, and windowsills.
There isn't much to do but wait
And watch as clear drops congregate
Then run to silver rivers on the glass.
It isn't long before that rippling view
Is not the pinesap-covered sled,
The sawhorse, or the rusted hoe and rake
That lean out back against the storage shed,
But rather some metallic ghost of me
Who also closes up his book and sits
Regardless of the rain that riddles him.
Does he remember, in Minnesota once,
The summer he was seventeen?
A struggling campfire whistled, popped, and hissed
As he and a girl named Caroline
Kissed until that fire embered out.
Above the massive spear tips of the pines,
Aurora borealis whipped and flared.
Though both of them were cold, neither cared.
And when she asked what he was thinking of,
He looked up at the wild sky and said
He didn't know, which was, of course, a lie.
But he was seventeen and couldn't say

That he felt very much in love,
Or that he was afraid to say goodbye.
So there they sat, stripped naked to the waist,
And watched the wrinkling, phosphorescent sky.

He's thirty-three, a little tired.
The fingers of a nearby cedar bough
Are weaving fragile ropes of rain
That ride the ridges of his brow.
Thinking of her, somewhere far away,
He knows the answer to that question now.

America the Beautiful

What patriotic boy could disagree
With Miss Vermont, who says she believes it's great
That after many years of fierce debate
The panel has reluctantly announced
That two-piece bathing suits will be allowed
In the swimwear competition? Before a crowd
Of journalists, she cocked her pretty head,
Fell deeply into a ruminative stare,
Then said, *I think, like totally, you know,*
It really brings our pageant up to date.
For some, the revolutionary road
Is wrought with angst. Along the cobbled way
We've lost our faith. The gods are gone.
The bathing beauties up on Helicon
Don't come around much anymore. But me,
I'm thinking progress isn't all half-bad,
Dressed in high, white heels, and bikini-clad.
And basically I totally concur
With Miss Vermont. I settle in to watch
As three tuxedoed judges squint and scrawl
While Miss Ohio bashfully admits
That romance novels, exercise, and prayer
Have kept her going these nerve-wracking months.
But when she hits the operatic note
In the orchestral, sorrowful, and long
Rendition of that Stephen Foster song,
It's clear that Miss Kentucky gets my vote.
The television camera slowly zooms

To make hot stars of all her sparkling tears.
She's independent, proudly resolute.
She's weeping in a million living rooms
And liberated after all these years.

High School Reunion, 1998

One time, when we were all a little drunk,
We played this game, and Sarah Petrikoff,
Whom I had worshipped since the seventh grade,
Said, *Raise your hand if you have ever done
The lonely, bonely deed.* My face went hot,
And for a second every boy looked down.
Then Charlie jabbed his fat, pink, stubby palm
Above his head, and when he understood
He'd been the only one to raise his hand,
We roared. I never liked him much but still,
This harrowed up my soul, froze my young blood,
And maybe—*maybe*—for a little while
He didn't seem so bad.

Outside the public swimming pool one night,
As Sarah leaned against my car, she touched
My arm. There was a vagrant breath of pine
And honeysuckle, the notion of chlorine,
My own repulsive sweat and her wet hair,
Still flowery with the scent of her shampoo.
I felt a tug—a slow, decisive rise—
And when I finally thought to close my eyes,
Lean in to her large breasts, and kiss her mouth,
Her boyfriend came to pick her up. He honked.
She told me I was cute, and *that*, as some
More seasoned veterans might say, was that.

I saw her late last June.
Reunion. Country Club. She'd put on weight,
Was still a little cruel, which was, I'm sure,

What made her seem so sexy back in school.
Out on the clubhouse balcony, balloons—
Each printed with our graduation year—
Grew tired and flabby in the breeze. A wedge
Of husky copper light began to slice
Across the carpet of the practice green.

Some had grown sleek and wealthy, others wise,
Though some had never really changed at all.
Take Charlie Taft. He leaned against the bar
In khaki slacks, buffed loafers, and a tie,
Blue-blazered like a dapper school boy still.
Soft spotlights warmed the CHAMPIONS' TROPHIES case,
As Charlie's fatter, slightly redder face
Grew moony in the antique afterglow
Of that immaculately printless glass,
The rich mahogany, and polished brass.
The Yiddish members of our class, he said,
They bitch about this place. Like they don't have
Exclusive Jew-clubs of their own. He thumbed
His butane lighter, lit a cigarette,
Then warped and blurred behind a veil of smoke.
He's got a wife and daughter, still lives in town.
He owns a big construction outfit now.
Scratch golfer. Father. Deacon. Boss. The kid
That I remembered from those years ago,
One night when we were all a little drunk
When I had thought to raise my hand as well,
But only briefly so.

O, Florida

This is the old country,
A land of statuary herons,
Where chevron squads of pelicans patrol
The glittering green shallows of the gulf.
Where color schemes are chiefly melon,
Flamingo pinks, and tropical pastels.
Where all day single-engine planes buzz by.
Their block red-letter advertisements scroll
Across those beefy, milk-white cumuli:
EAT SHRIMP AT RUBY'S-BY-THE-BAY.
RAW BAR AT JACK'S. ALASKA KING CRAB CLAWS.
ENJOY WORLD FAMOUS KEY LIME PIE.
Ponce de León, is this that paradise
You sought, whose tonics might restore
The potency and thrust of youth? The truth
Is that the old grow older here.
Their bones go frail as balsawood.
Strokes slur their speech. Their eyes become
Diminished lakes. We watch them dodder
Down grocery aisles. We see them heft
Their chronic coughs and aches along the beach.
Their sorrows all metastasize—they must—
And yet we seldom say a word
Or spend much time imagining ourselves
In thirty years. Shivering and sweating.
A lukewarm spittle on the chin.
Wide-open hours of waiting and regretting.
The air-conditioned room of our hotel
Looks out on swimming pool and sea.

We've paid good money for the view.
We seek the boredom that they know so well.

Back home, it's thirty-three degrees,
The March rain changing steadily to sleet.
We're only here another day. And if tonight
We eat at Ruby's-by-the-Bay
Or Jack's what difference will it make?
The beach boy, having closed up shop,
Has faced his bath chairs to the west
In regimented rows. Beside
The ponderous and receding tide
Three toasted, golden teenage girls relax.
They're sitting cross-legged in the sand
And posing for a picture that a fourth
Intends to take. Each tosses back her hair
Then feigns a fashion model's runway stare.
Cotton blouses. An almost chilly breeze.
That blush reflection of the sinking sun.
Just listen to them shriek and laugh.
Let memory and love arrest them there.

We've Gathered in a Formal Garden

We've gathered in a formal garden
Where all the boxwoods pose as leafy swans.
The fountain pumps its silver, frail bouquet,
And with a diamond-like panache
It scatters amulets and pendants
Where each of its eleven feeble jets
Begins to fray. The benefactors drink
Champagne. Their golden glasses seize
The early evening's lemon-colored light,
And cocktail chatter rarely goes beyond
The shrimp and crabmeat canapés.
But there are nods. Familiar sighs.
A cordial laugh about our host
Who, though he's in the bag, insists
On taking up the microphone to toast
These generous supporters of the cause.
His slurry, heartfelt words inspire
A thunderous concussion of applause
From brokers, lawyers, mostly monied men,
And all their handsome wives and dates.
Why lie? I'd somehow like to intimate
That I have, as of late, been shrewd,
That I foresaw the meteoric rise
In light sweet crude or rode the spike
Of cattle futures to the moon.
But what I know about the Middle East
Or the Guernsey herds in Iowa
Could hardly pave the way to Easy Street.
The purpling cloud-swirls churn and yeast.
And nighttime's first faint pinprick star

Begins, however meekly, to appear
Two inches off the shell-pink ear
Of Hartley Singer, a nice enough alum,
Who tells me when he studied here
The school was better. Only men.
Just six fraternities. The deans,
They understood that boys will be boys.
He shifts his weight, obliterates the star
And glances at the jazz quartet.
He gestures to the black man on guitar.
Another thing. Don't get him wrong.
But everyone was closer then.
There was this colored woman, cleaned their dorm.
She brought hot chicken broth when they were sick,
Asked every day about their grades.
She treated them like they were sons.
Before each Christmas break he'd send a card.
He'd slip a twenty-dollar bill inside
And write a note. He'd even sign it "love."
He'd fallen out of touch, you know.
A few homecomings back, his thirty-year,
He remembers it like yesterday,
Out on that dog-leg seventh hole,
He heard that she had passed away.
That night, when he was back at his motel,
He drank a whiskey, then he cried.
He blubbered like a little boy,
More than he had when his own mother died.
Things change, he says, and I agree.
Then Hartley Singer turns to find the bar.
And in the time it takes to notice
How the fountain's constant waters sound

Like static or an April's chilly rain,
I also notice I'm alone.
No, nothing quite at all like that,
Not sad or hurt or self-obsessed,
But just a little awkward in the crowd
Where conversation suddenly goes loud
With laughter, serious with drink.
Imagine, Hartley Singer, how the snow
Will cake this garden when the winter comes.
The ice will choke the fountain's alto voice
And all of summer's leaves we see
Will be forgotten in appalling sums.
It is the sorrow Adam understood.
Collect your wife. Fumble for your keys.
Remember where you parked the car.
Grow lonesome in the half-senilities
Of laughter, love, and early autumn's light,
And think how we will always seem so far,
So very far from home.

After Entertaining

As candled shadows spar along the hall
You clear the peppermill, the salad plates,
And latticework remains of whole, grilled trout.
You sponge the table and snuff the wicks,
Then leave the kitchen mess for morning.
The husband, nicest guy but dreadfully dull.
Turning up the second flight of stairs
You pause on the landing, looking out
At how the neighbor's floodlight overwhelms
His pachysandra and his ivied walls—
Those old, arthritic branches of his elms.
Her summer tan. A little slimmer then.
That almost indiscretion one July.
Nothing happened and nothing ever will.
Her husband. Dreadfully dull but the nicest guy.
And when you sidle in beside your wife
You breathe the fragrance of her soap, her sleep.
You sidle in beside your waking wife
And merely say, the Stocktons, dear, have gone.

Sea Glass

Two bankers drunkenly explain to me
That surf can grind a jagged piece of glass
Down to a smooth stone in an hour. One cocks
The hammer of a twenty-two and fires.
The other runs to get a second box
Of whiskey bottles and old jelly jars.
The clouds above Nantucket seem to stall
In one great, endless, anchored argosy
That treads the pale, blue surface of the sky,
And these two boys are thinking, overall,
That life is pretty good. They smoke cigars.
Between them they share bourbon from a flask.
Our conversation is thin. I do not ask
If they, by chance, had noticed driving in
The blood-rich glow of the cranberry bogs.
Nor do I call their brief attentions to
This old boneyard of salt-bleached driftwood logs.
I nod instead and quietly agree,
If what they've said about the tide is true,
That there is a ferocious skill to the sea.
I'd like to tell them that they're full of crap
But, it seems, they think I'm an OK guy,
And why ruin a good day out, I figure.
Besides, our girlfriends get along so well.
The brittle crack of rifle-fire is muted
In the rough wind as amber bottles rise
Then totter on the sleek and briefly fluted
Brims of the waves. These fellows mostly miss,
Though when they strike there is a puny spray
Of razors and bright amulets. Talk turns

From stocks to politics, then college lore,
And how one wild, intoxicated night,
Some pledges from the Kappa house next door
Had coaxed a girl who'd had too much to drink
Up to an empty room on their fourth floor.
Get this, the banker says. *They strip her down.*
They kill the lights, then every pledge lines up
To take their turns at her. This one kid shows
A little late. He's loaded, right? It's dark.
He screws this babe, and when he hits the switch
Finds out that it's his sister, who'd come up
For "Little Siblings' Weekend" at the school.
A seagull vehemently plucks and stabs,
At scallop shells and vacant claws of crabs
Along the water's vacillating edge.
The puckered face on banker number two,
Who aims the polished barrel at the sea,
Contorts a little more. *That's sick,* he says,
Of all the women I would want to rape
My sister is the last. Ten years from now
We'll vaguely recognize each others' names.
Our girlfriends may have married different men.
Across the tidal pond, the wind inscribes
Whole paragraphs in Braille. The bourbon is gone,
The bullets too. We drive our way back in.
Already on the ocean's supple floor,
A hundred puzzle parts of broken glass
Begin their figuration into stones.

On Having Said Something Cruel

Imagine Helen on the sun-bright bow
As she was spirited away
Through filaments of rainbow in the spray,
Through lacy counterpanes of foam.
She might have guessed the thrill could never last,
Or that her suitor would not always be
A dashing, doting, love-struck boy.

But who among those mortals could foresee
The bloody decade lost at Troy,
Their swift ship lunging headlong home,
The sea behind them in their sunlit wake
A gold and copper scattering of coins,
Extravagantly spent like so much love
Or all the bastard sons of Priam's loins?

Moving (Again)

Trimmed hedges, flower beds, and the groomed lawns
Grow smaller in the silver of the mirror.
The neighbors waving from their grim garage,
They, too, diminish first, then disappear.
They will go on about their busy lives.
They'll trim the hedge. They'll clean the grim garage.
Those old friends will continue grilling out.
They'll drink the frosty beer at sunset
As the great tectonic plates of August bronze
Slide quietly to nightshade on their lawns.

There will be talk and gossip just the same
While I, some several states away, begin
To read the long last chapter of a book,
Or walk the dog, or settle in for sleep.
Who knows what they will say. I should suppose
That they will mention me. And I may be,
To some, a fondly recollected thought.
Good-humored. Well-respected. Loyal.
Though in the grillsmoke-sweetened summer dusk,
To others, surely not.

IV

Bill Fowler's Pointer Hears a Voice

It says he craves the taste of squirrel,
Of rabbit and black snake, even wasp.
It tells him that the scum-choked pond
Is a delicious drink. *The air*
And earth, it says, *are languages,*
And you must ponder what they mean.
Wild peppermint, the sassafras,
Larkspur, trillium, the squandered salt,
The hidden, urinary script
On leaves, on wrappers, bark, and weeds.
It tells him that he is a god
Whose rolling golden agate eyes
Reveal an inward fire. I've seen
Him when the voice has stopped him flat
In his exquisite stride and said
Forget the squirrel, the luscious wasp.
Inhale this ripe bouquet instead:
The unapologetic, pure
Cologne of carrion. Or this:
The dark, sweet essences of shit.
Breathe deep, it says, *think twice, then drive*
Your bony shoulder into it.

Watching Nature on TV

The hare, the meadow mouse, and squirrel
Have grown remarkably at ease,
Considering the Cooper's hawk
That rides a cool and inviolate arc.
She dips. She sideslips on the breeze.
She cries out loud that they should *Fear!*
And yet they do not seem to hear.
These ardent creatures of the field
That rush but never quite arrive,
That gaze though never truly see,
They eat the acorn's meat, the chive,
The garden parsnip, and the peach.
All seems so peaceful in their soft
And muzzy little lives. But I
Have seen this episode, and know
That any moment now the squirrel
Will feel a sudden, violent spike.
He will be tackled, trundled off,
Then relished in a private glade.
His death will be replayed for us
At slow and gruesome speeds. He will
Become a silver slump of fur,
The blood flecks on the raptor's beak.
Memento mori. Shortly, though,
We'll turn our thoughts to lighter things—
A pouty grizzly cub that stalks
The pink, metallic salmon as they spawn.
Clark's grebe, which bloats his gullet when he sings.
We'll travel to the piney north
And watch the slapstick back-and-forth

Of otters in their spangled lake.
But children, all the while the prairies ache.
Night falling on the mouse and hare,
The coal-fire eyes of cats and foxes stare
For brittle matchstick rustlings in the brush.
An owl in dark, carved marble stillness waits
High on his twisted branch somewhere.

Probability and Statistics

Go figure Schmidt. A three-martini swell.
An actuary on the seventh floor
Of Babcock's firm. He's twice divorced, likes cats,
And always has a seed-pearl chain of sweat
Across his upper lip. A regular guy.
Well, anyway, to look at him, you'd think
He's nothing sly. A smidgen overweight,
Perhaps. His teeth somewhat tobacco stained.
But still, he makes the tipsy ladies laugh.
Besides, he likes to joke, it rarely hurts—
The lamps on low, and Heaven bless the smoke!
To him, it's nothing ventured, nothing gained,
And we like him well enough, but make our bets
On when he'll go too far. We watch him prowl
His prospects at the bar—grim waitresses
And secretary types in double-knits.
If Schmidt has taught us anything it's this:
That one should never underestimate
The gin-persuaded optics of the eye,
Or how, near closing time, the heart grows primed
For compromise. And Christ! sometimes it works,
Though what he says is anybody's guess.
A whiff of cocktail onions on his breath.
Half whisper in the juniper dark, half slur.
Sometimes, a really pleasant girl says *Yes*.

Aubade

The poet on the cover of the book
Has scowled at me, it seems, for months.
He's cast a mean, unblinking, stony look

As if eternally to say,
Listen! you prying, measly mouse
Think what you like, there shall be no surprise.

There shall be no deception here. Two weeks
Of reading and it's true. Today
Before my breakfast Philip Larkin dies

As lonely as I somehow knew he would.
What good could come of it,
To read the sad last chapter of a life

By lamplight as the gauzy dawn
Is ushered in by a warbler's song?
It's just too depressing some will say.

Perhaps they're right. What kind of way
Is that to start an April day?
Although his ending tends to make things clear.

The coffee cools. Outside the hills are spiked
With timid shafts of daffodils,
And all the knuckling, waxy buds

Have jeweled the geriatric limbs of trees.
If Larkin be at restlessness or peace,
I couldn't half begin to tell.

For now, the certainties are small:
Two saber blades of sunlight knife
Along the tiles of the kitchen floor.

The eggs are sizzling in the skillet grease,
I've got fresh juice, sweet butter on my toast,
And an absolutely boring peach preserve—

On any average day I mostly know,
It never hurts to be reminded though,
How excellent it is to be alive.

The Dandelions

They've woken up miraculously old,
Not swinesnout now or cankerwort,
Not teeth of lions scattered on the lawn,
But silver geodesic ghosts
Where yesterday they stood as common coins
Of summer's gold. In flowerbeds
And terra cotta pots, in the cracks
Of sidewalks, patios, and drives
They nod their sleepy cobweb heads
As if they've listened and are strangely swayed
By something that they used to loathe or fear.
These two, for instance, in the windowbox.
The few there in that cold crab-apple shade.
Sad step of time. Such memories like lace.
Some hover, lost as sudden blooms
Of August frost among the lavender
And hollyhocks, staggering underneath
Our summer's green, relentless pace.

Ripeness Is All

Our nightmare has begun.
The windows of the elementary school
Are terrible with black
Construction paper cats
And overlarge arachnids
Knitting webs of orange yarn.
The jigsaw shapes of witches
Cruise the wide fluorescent air
Above our produce aisles.
And over at the firehouse,
They've hung three sheets—
Those benevolent and boneless dead—
That float there more like misplaced jellyfish
Than anything that might
Suggest a soul.

Each Halloween
Our one-time maven of the Junior League,
Esther Gibbons, waits
At the end of her dark lane.
No children ever venture there
Though she'll still keep a basket filled
With nickels by her door, a jar
Of antique butterscotch.
Who remembers anymore
The taste of her blue-ribbon oyster stew,
Or the maraschino ruby tinge
Of her manhattans?
They're mostly gone, those citizens
Who smoked their Chesterfields

And drank, who richly spent
Their summer evenings
Relaxing on her candled, crew-cut lawn.

You can almost begin to see,
In all its nineteenth-century despair,
Her cracked-white coveted estate.
It rots behind a scrim
Of gingko golds and sugar-maple reds.
Every month it seems
Another millionaire
Has offered her a handsome price.
She will not sell. Her property
Instead falls further into ill repair.
Clematis fingers at its throat.
Her columns writhe
In osteoperotic pain.

October in a presidential year,
And the pharmacist has taken sides.
"Free speech!" he likes to say.
His shopfront glows
With jack-o-lanterns and election signs.
His eyes like blue aluminum,
A fat, red cherub's face, his hair
The brittle sheen of hay. These nights
His well-waxed Lincoln haunts
The lot behind the Shriners' lodge.
Gossip suggests
His no-contest divorce.
A week from now his brash conservatives
Will surely sweeps the polls.

I am a Democrat myself,
Unfortunately prone
To long periods of doubt.
I am a widower and ex-
Accountant for the state whose modest
Though sufficient salary paid
The mortgage on a single-story ranch.
There were vacations to the beach,
Weekends to the country,
And even, once, a Caribbean cruise.
Out in the den you'll find
Four decades' worth of photographs.
It is a dustless, bright
Chronology of Christmas eves
And Easter afternoons, sunburns,
Saltwater taffy stands,
Brand, spanking new sedans,
Luxuriously frosted wedding cakes,
And relatives who mostly stopped
En route to somewhere else.
As if each glad occasion,
Each happy instant in our lives,
Could be preserved by Polaroid
And neatly trapped beneath
The cellophane, protective sleeves
Of a Sears & Roebuck picture album.

At least it was a merciful decline,
Untreatable, astonishingly swift,
And in the end, for her,
An anesthesia-softened dream.
One Friday she was diagnosed

And less than four weeks later, gone.
So we escaped the years-long marathon
Of therapies and false-reliefs,
The prolonged pursuit and cost
Of expert medical advice.
And now, eleven seasons
After she has passed, I have
More money than a man like me
Could ever hope to spend.

Tomorrow after dusk they will appear,
The freshly laundered little ghosts,
Gunslingers, and the pink
Carnation-colored fairy queens.
A small chaos of skeletons and clowns
Will knuckle at the door.
Then gradually a second wave.
The slightly older, mischievous,
Unchaperoned, and bored.
Throwers of rotten eggs
And the Charmin-armed
Redecorators of our oaks.
First morning of November will reveal
A ghastly misdemeanor spree—
The crushed and grinning skulls
Of pumpkins on our stoops,
Obscenities in Ivory Soap.
I'm afraid one learns to grow resigned.

Just look at our forsaken courthouse square.
A clock whose rusted guts
Have grinded to a halt.

The businesses are spare.
What's left? A florist and a hair salon,
The used appliance store
And Casper's luncheonette,
Where more and more I tend
To find myself at noon, and where,
From one of several window seats,
You can glimpse the strict
And rigid form of Robert Edward Lee,
"The Marble Monument,"
Our alabaster patron saint.

And pinioned there a little bit like Christ,
Two giant asterisks for eyes,
A kindly Botticelli nod,
The scarecrow at the bank who waits
In autumn's chilly padlock gray
And neither grieves nor celebrates
Another shriveling year.
He merely stares instead
Down stately Olive Avenue,
Whose canopy of shade has thinned
To a high-branching herringbone,
Where late last Monday night,
In the strange, rainless wallop of the wind,
Our sheriff found her naked and alone,
Bewildered Mrs. Gibbons,
In tattered gardening gloves
And a pair of yellow rubber boots,
An old corroded pitchfork in her hands.

In Here. Out There.

These acorns from the storm-tormented tree
Rain down a madness overhead,
Exploding intermittently,
As if they'd wake the lazy dead.
But it's three a.m.
And nothing now is rousing them.
It's only me instead
Who hears the rapid hammerwork,
That wrathful smack of seed against the roof.
And it is clear,
To draw the curtain back
And scan my tranquil street from here,
That all or most are still at rest.
There doesn't seem to be a reading lamp
Or a faint, blue television glow
In all the houses down the row.
No, they've chosen different shade.
Maple. Maybe pine.
I'm certain they're not sleeping under oaks.
But surely, if they were,
They'd understand this desire of mine,
To take a freshly sharpened axe,
To rage and split,
And take each meaty log,
Halve and quarter it,
Then cinder each last log to ash.
I'd watch that tree
Ride skyward in its noiseless smoke,
On a night like this, high wind and fog,
Until that oak,

And all my raging too, would seem
The blowsy substance of a dream.
A mile away,
Someone—it may be you—might catch the spice
Of wood smoke on the moist air
And think, or even start to say
To someone else, how nice
The night would go beside a fire.
You wouldn't spend a thought
On why that fire came to be,
And scarcely could you comprehend the plot—
Acorns and acorns
Shaken from their tree,
Beating on the brain of one
Who turns his sleepless, inward-looking eye
On failures and regrets.
His doubts, his sorrows, they multiply
As ragged fog banks bluster by.
He hears not just the wind's
And oak's commotion in his ears,
But woeful, stupid, half-cocked things
He's sometimes said.
Glass rattling in the gust.
Warp and boom. Sway and bow.
He has had enough
Of worry's calculus for now,
And of the oak tree's nightmare head.
Already from his tossed and twisted bed
He notices the way
The blue-blackness in his window
Has started pearling into gray.
It won't be long—

The night will soften into sallow dawn,
And then he won't think much of fire,
The axe, the varnish of its helve, or you.
He'll listen as those north-
By-northwest gales begin to die,
As all such weathers do.
He may feel troubled for a day,
Perhaps a few,
To see the first of cold October's leaves
Spun up and scattered
On the ashen sky,
Hearing a boot sole scuffing on the walk,
Or raw bitching of a crow's cry.

First Frost

Man in this state is nothing but a unit of quantity,
an occupied moment of time.

Schiller

A dust has settled over us.
The jack-o-lanterns on the sugared lawns
Look stricken with surprise. The crows discuss
The chill with a predictable contempt.
In the park, an icy melanoma grows
Across the bridge of Friedrich Schiller's nose.
He loiters in the garden, cast in bronze.

The mallards paddle through a fine steam
As if their concrete pool were piping hot.
Cold curls of vapor twist and rise. This dream,
This glazed and brittle vision will dissolve
Before our eyes. Enameled windshield glass
Will thaw. Each nickel-plated blade of grass,
Each crystal shrub and chilled forget-me-not

Will soon be jeweled and fresh with wet.
The brassy sunlight angling through the oak
Will soften Schiller's cancer into sweat.
We know but will not say just what this is
That has so elegantly capped and pearled
The fringes, flats, and corners of our world.
We see it also in the stony smoke

Of our evaporating breath
That plumes and billows in the morning glare.
We know but will not say that this is death.
Come lunchtime in the mellow, midday heat,
Some will feel mournful though they may not weep.
A few will think primarily of sleep
And taste it in the sweetly appled air.

Poetry Titles in the Series

John Hollander, *Blue Wine and Other Poems*
Robert Pack, *Waking to My Name: New and Selected Poems*
Philip Dacey, *The Boy under the Bed*
Wyatt Prunty, *The Times Between*
Barry Spacks, *Spacks Street, New and Selected Poems*
Gibbons Ruark, *Keeping Company*
David St. John, *Hush*
Wyatt Prunty, *What Women Know, What Men Believe*
Adrien Stoutenberg, *Land of Superior Mirages: New and
    Selected Poems*
John Hollander, *In Time and Place*
Charles Martin, *Steal the Bacon*
John Bricuth, *The Heisenberg Variations*
Tom Disch, *Yes, Let's: New and Selected Poems*
Wyatt Prunty, *Balance as Belief*
Tom Disch, *Dark Verses and Light*
Thomas Carper, *Fiddle Lane*
Emily Grosholz, *Eden*
X. J. Kennedy, *Dark Horses: New Poems*
Wyatt Prunty, *The Run of the House*
Robert Phillips, *Breakdown Lane*
Vicki Hearne, *The Parts of Light*
Timothy Steele, *The Color Wheel*
Josephine Jacobsen, *In the Crevice of Time: New and
    Collected Poems*
Thomas Carper, *From Nature*
John Burt, *Work without Hope: Poetry by John Burt*
Charles Martin, *What the Darkness Proposes: Poems*
Wyatt Prunty, *Since the Noon Mail Stopped*
William Jay Smith, *The World below the Window: Poems 1937–1997*
Wyatt Prunty, *Unarmed and Dangerous: New and
    Selected Poems*
Robert Phillips, *Spinach Days*
X. J. Kennedy, *The Lords of Misrule: Poems 1992–2001*
John T. Irwin, ed., *Words Brushed by Music: Twenty-Five
    Years of the Johns Hopkins Poetry Series*
John Bricuth, *As Long As It's Big: A Narrative Poem*
Robert Phillips, *Circumstances Beyond Our
    Control: Poems*
Daniel Anderson, *Drunk in Sunlight*